SUMMARY

TO

D1826521

Morning Star

Pierce Brown

TRIVIA EDITION COLLECTION

By WhizBooks

Before We Begin

Dear reader,

To say thank you,

We've included a free gift download of our *All-Time Top 5 Bestselling* Guides for you absolutely free.

To access your free bonus gifts enter your email for an instant delivery of our *All-Time Top 5 Bestselling* titles to your inbox.

Enter Best Email Address Here

We hope you will enjoy this book. Don't forget to keep score, and then challenge your friends and family.

What will your trivia score be?

Editor at
WhizBooks

Table of Contents

Round One: Set Go

"Ready to start the challenge?"

1 POINT EACH

Question #1

At the time of the Second Moon Lords' Rebellion, how many planets of the solar system fell under the jurisdiction of the Sovereign?

a. 1

b. 3

c. 4

d. 5

3

The novel opens with a picture of the solar system showing the planetary systems and overlords who govern them. Earth, Venus, and Mercury are together referred to as the Loyalists because they are all aligned with the Sovereign of the Society, Octavia of House Lune. Mars stands alone under the guardianship of its Arch-Governor, Adrius au Augustus, (codenamed **The Jackal**) of House Augustus. Jupiter, Saturn, Uranus, Neptune, and Pluto have all together declared their independence.

Question #2

What was the name of Darrow's murdered wife?

    a. Mustang

    b. Julian

    c. Lorn

    d. Eo

ANSWER d

Eo

Darrow was born a Red, living the life of a lowly miner below the surface of Mars until the death of his wife changed the status quo. Eo, Darrow's wife (whom he loved dearly) was hanged for inciting rebellion. Darrow then teamed up with the revolutionary group, the Sons of Ares, to correct the flaws inherent in their existence as the lowest of the low. A physical transformation changes Darrow into a Gold, and the quest to turn the Society on its head from the inside, sees Darrow in a tangled love affair with a Gold,

Virginia au Augustus, twin sister to Adrius the Jackal.

Question #3

What word replaces the concept of heaven/paradise in the novel?

    a. Vale

    b. Lykos

    c. Attica

    d. Palatine Hill

ANSWER a

Vale

Darrow is on the verge of being broken by his imprisonment. He longs for death to free him. But he says, "…the more I see of this cruel world, the less I believe it ends in some pleasant fiction. The Vale is not real." He goes on to say that the Vale "is a lie told by mothers and fathers to give their starving children a reason for the horror." A debate rages on in his brain, contesting a place of limitless pleasantness beyond this plane called the Vale.

Question #4

Why does the Jackal hand over Darrow to Aja and her Carvers for dissection?

    a. To torture him into servitude

    b. To humiliate him before his loved ones

    c. To find out how he, a Red, became a Gold

    d. To find the source of his fortitude

ANSWER c

To find out how he, a Red, became a Gold

D arrow had been born a Red but took up the semblance of a Gold so he could infiltrate their ranks and destroy them from within. Now captured, his captors sought to unveil the secret of his imposture. The Sons of Ares had with them the secret that turned Reds to Golds. And the Jackal and his allies believed that dissecting the body of Darrow would provide the answer to the nagging question of how he'd successfully been made one of them.

Who among the allies of the Jackal does not approve of the spectacle of a tortured Darrow?

    a. Antonia

    b. Cassius

    c. Zanzibar

    d. Lilath

ANSWER b

Cassius

Present for the presentation of a tortured and nearly broken Darrow at the Attica hall of Adrius, the Jackal, were Aja, of House Grimmus, Antonia, Thistle, Cassius, Lilath, and Calliope. Cassius is of House Bellona, and although an enemy to Darrow, he sees no point in the inhuman torture and exhibition that the Jackal, of House Augustus, is reveling unashamedly in. When the servants fail to do his bidding of fetching a blanket to cover Darrow, Cassius stripes off his cloak and drapes it over Darrow.

Question #6

Who are the two Grays that free Darrow from the Carvers?

    a. Holiday and Trigg

    b. Danto and Sevro

    c. Cassius and Mickey

    d. Ragnar and Dancer

ANSWER a

Holiday and Trigg

oliday ti Nakamura and her younger sibling, Triggti Nakamura are Grays who are legionnaires. They are commissioned by the remnants of the Sons of Ares to rescue Darrow, the Reaper. They are brave and intelligent, taking calculated risks that tilt the balance in their favor. Nonetheless, Trigg fails to make it past the extraction point. He's cut down by Aja au Grimmus, who "spears him through the torso with her razor," just as they near the extraction point after activating Plan C.

Once upon a time, _____ made necklaces of

ears.

a. Titus

b. Sevro

c. Vixus

d. Antonia

ANSWER c

Vixus

During the escape from the cadaver rooms deep in the prison bowels of the Jackal where Aja's carvers were working to unveil the secret that turned Darrow, a lowly Red, into Darrow, the Reaper Gold, Trigg, Holiday, and Darrow ride a gravLift towards their "evac" point. They are joined by Vixus au Serna, a lieutenant of the Boneriders. Vixus is a ruthless soldier who used to make necklaces of ears from the enemies he had slain in warfare.

What informed the diversion from the initial escape route?

    a. Trigg wants to play the hero.

    b. Holiday wants to create more chaos.

    c. Darrow needs to save a friend.

    d. The gravLift in which they are riding malfunctions.

ANSWER c

Darrow needs to save a friend.

Darrow, the Reaper found out from Vixus au Serna after the ensuing fracas in the gravLift that Victra au Julii, half-sister of Antonia au Severus-Julli, was still alive but held as a captive on level 23 cell 2187. Although going to free Victra entailed getting too far off from the "evac" point, Darrow felt he owed her that much. Victra had risked so much for him and would go as far as dying for him. He simply wasn't about to leave her behind, knowing the hideous things her captors were capable of doing to her.

Question #9

Who betrayed Darrow to the Jackal?

a. Roque

b. Sevro

c. Lilath

d. Cassius

ANSWER a

Roque

Sevro au Barca was a lieutenant of the Sons of Ares alongside Ragnar Volarus, Dancer, Mickey, and Darrow. He was responsible for the mission undertaken by Trigg and Holiday to rescue Darrow. He was a trusted friend who could never betray Darrow. Lilath au Faran, the leader of the Boneriders, was the companion of Adrius, the Jackal. Her path and Darrow's could not yield a betrayal. Roque au Fabii, Imperator of the Sword of Armada was the "Judas" in the equation that saw Darrow and the Sons of Ares betrayed.

Question #10

What were the instruments of Victra's torture?

    a. Forceps and scalpels

    b. Carving knives and electrocutions

    c. Sound and light

    d. Drugs and water

ANSWER c

Sound and light

Darrow's torture has involved the physical instruments of scalpels, carving knives, drugs, water, and a host of others. They were used to tear away his flesh, inflicting physical trauma to weaken any vestiges of a resolve to stay unbroken by the torture. Victra au Julli, after being shot in the spine by her half-sister Antonia au Severus-Julii, was given the torture of lights and sounds; the exact opposite of Darrow's abuse at the hands of his merciless captors.

Round Two: Getting Harder

"Let's get personal."

2 POINTS EACH

Question #1

In what year did author, Pierce Brown, graduate from college?

  b. 1988

  c. 1999

  d. 2010

  e. 2014

Born on Thursday, January 28, 1988, to influential and powerful CEO mother, Colleen Brown (of the Fisher Communications' fame), novelist Pierce Brown is an only child. Now 28 years old, Pierce Brown graduated college at 22 years old (in 2010) from the private, coeducational research university established in 1937 in affiliation with the Churches of Christ, called the Pepperdine University (formerly George Pepperdine College) situated in Malibu. With an endowment fund of some 805.2 USD in 2015, the

University has been ranked 52nd by U.S News & World Report's 2016 ranking.

Question #2

In what year did the author win the Goodreads Choice Award for Best Debut Goodreads Author?

    a. 2016

    b. 2015

    c. 2014

    d. 2013

In 2014, Pierce Brown was voted the winner of the Goodreads Choice Awards for Best Debut Goodreads Author for the novel *Red Rising,* the first in the Red Rising Trilogy. It was a contest keenly contested by brilliant debut authors like Mary Kubica (of *The Good Girl* fame), Andy Wier (author of *The Martian*), Danielle Paige (*Dorothy Must Die*), Danielle L. Jensen (*Stolen Songbird*), Rosemund Hodge (*Cruel Beauty*), and others, who were nominated for the award.

Question #3

What novel was nominated as a Goodreads Choice Awards for Best Young Adult Fantasy & Science Fiction?

    a. Red Rising

    b. Golden Son

    c. Morning Star

    d. Iron Gold

ANSWER a

Red Rising

Having won the Goodreads Choice Awards for Best Debut Goodreads Author in 2014, Pierce Brown was also a strong contending nominee for the Goodreads Choice Awards for Best Young Adult Fantasy & Science Fiction with his novel, the *Red Rising*. Cassandra Clare won that category of award with her novel, *City of Heavenly Fire*. On the honor row of nominees include Tahereh Mafi, with *Ignite Me*, Ransom Riggs, with *Hollow City,* and Sarah J. Maas, with *Heir of Fire*.

Question #4

What was the occupation of Pierce Brown's father?

    a. Accountant

    b. Banker

    c. Stock Broker

    d. Screenwriter

ANSWER b

Banker

Pierce Brown is the only child of a banker called Guy Brown and a business administrator called Colleen Brown. Pierce's father, Guy Brown, together with Pierce's high society mother, Colleen Brown, raised their lone son in seven different states. This was occasioned primarily by the parents' job demands. However, young Pierce had a lot of fun growing up with his cousins on both parents' side. He and his cousins played rough and tumble in a game of wits as they set traps for each other.

Question #5

What were the majors of the author's bachelor's degree program?

a. Banking and Finance

b. Creative Writing and English

c. Political Science and Economics

d. Economics and Mathematics

ANSWER c

Political Science and Economics

At 18 years old, when Pierce Brown gained admission to Pepperdine University, he enrolled to major in political science and economics. This choice may well be the influences his father and mother had on him in his formative years. Listening to his father and mother trade stories of boardroom politics at the supper table must have impressed the young Pierce. So too must have been the rich narrations of the economics behind financial decisions made in their respective fields of work.

Question #6

Where was Pierce Brown residing when he sold his first novel *Red Rising* in 2012?

    a. With his mother in Fairfax

    b. In the garage of his former college professor

    c. In the basement of a Senator's house

    d. With his girlfriend

ANSWER b

In the garage of his former college professor

After graduation from College, Pierce Brown had his fair share of stints working different jobs. It was during this period that the decision to venture into writing was made. While working in Burbank, California on the NBC Page Program, he wrote his first novel, *Red Rising*. He was able to sell it to the publisher at Del Rey (an imprint of Penguin Random House) while still living in the rusty old garage of his former college professor.

Question #7

How many rejection slips did the author garner before selling his first?

    a. Below 10

    b. Between 50 and 60

    c. Between 70 and 100

    d. Over 120

ANSWER d

Over 120

Many writers give up their dreams of writing after a few rejection slips from editors, but not Pierce Brown. He knew what persistence meant. With a whopping count of over one hundred and twenty rejection slips, he persisted until his book *Red Rising* saw the light of day. The book was an instant hit, peaking on *The New York Times* bestseller list at #20. The book received nominations and an award for the brilliant prose and plot twists woven by Pierce Brown.

Question #8

How many followers does the author have on Twitter?

a. 17.7K

b. 15.9K

c. 25.7K

d. 7K

Answer a

17.7K

Pierce Brown has been on Twitter since 2011 and has since been able to build his followership to the 17K mark. Although not exactly phenomenal, this young entrant into the dystopian world of Science Fiction is certainly gaining attention. He has managed nearly 7600 tweets with 182 photo/video uploads on the Twiter™ platform to date while promoting his Red Rising Trilogy works with the public. His followership on Facebook is in the five figures region; again, not bad for an "upstart."

Question #9

In a tweet by the author, what is the answer to the question posed by his friend: "Your house is so incredibly clean. Did your maid come today?"

a. "No, my mum visited."

b. "Yup, she did."

c. "No. I have a book deadline."

d. "No. My girlfriend helped."

ANSWER c

"No. I have a book deadline."

The author associates extreme productivity with cleanliness and order. We see this in a tweet that simultaneously poses a question by a "friend" and the author's response of "No. I have a book deadline." to the question. The tweet is hilarious as it is informative on the writer's working ethic and core belief in the factors of productivity. He assumes responsibility for his environment while hinting at its importance in getting him committed to meeting deadlines.

Question #10

How long did the author take to complete the *Red Rising* manuscript?

    a. 2 years

    b. 2 months

    c. 10 months

    d. 1 year

ANSWER b

2 months

Once he convinced himself of his storytelling abilities, Pierce Brown sank into the task of writing his first Sci-Fi novel while boarding at his parents' house in Seattle. He reports that it took him the better part of two consecutive months to get it all out– taking sleep deprivation to an unprecedented level in its redefinition. He tells of how his muses were in overdrive, helping him to enjoy the chore of articulating the sequence of plot outplay into the cinematic masterpiece it turn out to be in the end.

Reminder: Claim Your Books

Dear reader,

If you haven't already, don't forget to claim your free download of our *All-Time Top 5 Bestselling* Guides for you absolutely free as a part of this purchase.

Just enter where you want the books to be digitally delivered.

Enter Best Email Address Here

We hope you will enjoy this book.

What will your trivia score be?

Editor at
WhizBooks

Round Three: Enter Fan Zone

"Are you a true fan?"

3 POINTS EACH

Question #1

To whose novel does *Kirkus Reviews* compare the plot outplay in *Morning Star*?

    a. Frank Herbert's *Dune*

    b. Neal Stephenson's *Seveneves*

    c. Victoria Aveyard's *Red Queen*

    d. Brandon Sanderson's *Firefight*

ANSWER a

Frank Herbert's *Dune*

Niall Alexander's review of the *Morning Star* in TOR.COM's book reviews claimed that Pierce Brown "has several times cited *Star Wars* as an influence." He likens *Red Rising* to *A New Hope*, *Golden Son* to *The Empire Strikes Back*, and *Morning Star* to *Return of the Jedi*. The *Kirkus Review*, on the other hand, compared the "multilayered" plot of *Morning Star* to the "characters who exist in a shadow world between history and myth" of Frank Herbert's *Dune.*

What is the worst ranking any Red Rising Trilogy book has had on *The New York Times bessSeller* list?

a. #50

b. # 40

c. #30

d. #20

The writing career of Pierce Brown has blossomed remarkably since beating the odds in securing a publishing contract with Del Rey Books in 2012. When the first of the Red Rising Trilogy was released in 2014, it rose up the charts of *The New York Times* bestseller list to #20, its worst ever showing on the list. The second book in the trilogy, *Golden Son*, scored a peak hit at #6 in the following year of 2015. *Morning Star*, the third installment of the Red

Rising Trilogy clinched the #1 spot on both the *USA Today* and *The New York Times* bestseller lists in 2016.

Question #3

How many Goodreads Awards does the author have under his belt?

    a. 4

    b. 3

    c. 2

    d. 1

When Pierce Brown's *Red Rising* debuted in 2014, it "stole" the Goodreads Choice Award for Best Debut Goodreads Author, while simultaneously nominated for Best Yong Adult Fantasy & Science Fiction. In 2015, Pierce Brown won the Goodreads Choice Award for Best Science Fiction with the fast-paced cinematic, action-packed 2015 publication of the sequel to *Red Rising, Golden Son.* Thus far, Pierce Brown has won two important Goodreads Awards and has been nominated

in three categories.

What Pierce Brown novel won a nomination in 2014 for the Goodreads Choice Award for Best Young Adult Fantasy & Science Fiction?

    a. Morning Star

    b. Red Rising

    c. Golden Son

    d. Iron Gold

ANSWER b

Red Rising

Nominated alongside the Young Adult Fantasy & Science Fiction titles *City of Heavenly Fire, Ignite Me, Hollow City, Four: A Divergent Collection, The One, Silver Shadows: A Bloodlines Novel, Heir of Fire, Cress,* and *Dreams of Gods and Monsters,* Pierce Brown's book I of the Red Rising Trilogy was beaten into second place by Cassandra Clare's *City of Heavenly Fire*. But it was a good showing for a newcomer. As a consolation, the book would go on to win in another Goodreads Choice Awards category, namely Best Debut Goodreads Author.

Question #5

What Maximumpop (MP!) Bookish Awards has the *MorningStar* being nominated for?

    a. Fantasy/Sci-Fi Book of the year

    b. Book of the year

    c. Young Adult Book of the year

    d. E-Book of the year

Answer b

Book of the Year

Hodderscape @hodderscape tweeted, "@beckysaysrawr and @pierce_brown are up for #MPBookishAwards and YOU can help them win." The tweet had *The Long Way Up A Small Angry Planet* and the *Morning Star* nominated for Fantasy/Sci-Fi Book of the Year Award and Book of the Year Award respectively. Voting was ongoing at www.maximumpop.co.uk. Pierce Brown retweeted it on his Twittter™ handle the same day, complete with picture uploads of the nomination plaques.

In how many languages is The Red Rising Trilogy

available?

    a. Nearly 15

    b. Just 5

    c. Exactly 2

    d. Over 30

ANSWER d

Over 30

With popular critical acclaim comes a surge in sales and a clamor for translation into other languages for a wider reach in reading audience worldwide. So already basking in the euphoria of a successful debut outing with the publication of the Red Rising Trilogy, Pierce Brown's books have gained an ascendancy that is seeing them translated into more than 30 more languages in the short time span of their presence on book lists across the world.

How many pages are there in the Hardcover edition

of the *Morning Star* as published by Del Rey on

February 9, 2016?

a. 254

b. 524

c. 518

d. 581

Sever, page counts have been given for the book length of *Morning Star.* The five hundred and twenty-four-page count is reflective of the total leaves count in the hardcover edition, as distinct from the page count of the story itself, which stands at five hundred and eighteen. So, Wikipedia is right to cite five hundred and eighteen pages for it. Conversely, Amazon cites an ebook Kindle edition page count of five hundred and forty-six.

Question #8

What is the peak Amazon accolade for the book,

Morning Star?

a. An Amazon Best Book of February 2016

b. An Amazon Best ebook of 2016

c. An Amazon Best Sci-Fi Book of 2016

d. An Amazon Best Fantasy Book of 2016

ANSWER a

An Amazon Best Book of February 2016

Peaking at #1 on *The New York Times* bestseller list in 2016, *Morning Star* also peaked at #1 on the *USA Today* list. This sales performance helped it ace an accolade on Amazon as the Amazon Best Book of February 2016. Most readers who have reviewed *Morning Star* point to its lackluster dramatics when compared to its predecessor, *Golden Son*. Nevertheless, all agree that it provides a satisfying end to the Red Rising Trilogy.

Question #9

What is the difference in the star rating of *Morning Star* on Amazon and Goodreads?

a. 0.3

b. 0.29

c. 0.1

d. 0.2

ANSWER b

0.29

Goodreads rates *Morning Star* with a 4.51-star rating from 34,426 ratings and 4,196 reviews. Amazon scores it with a star rating of 4.8 stars out of 5 from 1,582 customer reviews. The difference in star ratings between the two platforms is decidedly 0.29 stars–signaling a close contest between the two. The difference also shows a consistency with the ratings and thus is a strong indicator of the genuineness of all the hype the book gained just before its release in February 2016, from the stables of Del Rey.

Question #10

Which movie production house has acquired the rights for a film adaptation of *Red Rising*?

    a. Universal Pictures

    b. 20th Century Fox

    c. Tristar Pictures

    d. Warner Bros

ANSWER a

Universal Pictures

Pierce Brown became an instant millionaire soon after the release of the *Red Rising* by Del Rey Books in 2016 when Universal Pictures bought the rights for its film adaptation with a price tag well into seven digits. The film adaptation is slated to be produced by Joe Roth under the directing genius of Marc Foster. The second and third installments of the trilogy have proven what a gifted author Pierce Brown is, and that no doubt factors into the investment decision by Universal Pictures in the procurement of the film adaptation rights.

The Moment of Truth

Results May Vary

Based on the difficulty of the questions you are an Avid Fan if you've scored more than "41" points.

Play Again?

The First Challenge

The Second Challenge

The Third Challenge

or

Go to Next Page

Last Chance

Dear reader,

If you haven't already, this is the last chance to download our *All-Time Top 5 Bestselling* Guides for you absolutely free for you absolutely free as a part of this purchase.

Just enter where you want the books to be digitally delivered.

Enter Best Email Address Here

We hope you have enjoyed this book. Please take a moment to leave a review of this book at the end and share your experience.

Editor at
WhizBooks

Lightning Source UK Ltd.
Milton Keynes UK
UKHW020643270519
343383UK00013B/1905/P

9 780464 993834